IMAGES
of America

WRENTHAM

C.E.P.
1897

IMAGES
of America

WRENTHAM

C. Gordon "Gog" Woodhams
and Earle T. Stewart

ARCADIA
PUBLISHING

Published by Arcadia Publishing
Charleston, South Carolina

Library of Congress Catalog Card Number: 9962636

For all general information contact Arcadia Publishing at:
Telephone 843-853-2070
Fax 843-853-0044
E-mail sales@arcadiapublishing.com
For customer service and orders:
Toll-Free 1-888-313-2665

Visit us on the Internet at www.arcadiapublishing.com

CONTENTS

ACKNOWLEDGMENTS

The authors wish to thank all of the individuals who serve or have ever served on the Wrentham Historical Commission and all of those people who have contributed pictures to the commission for the more than 30 years that it has been in existence.

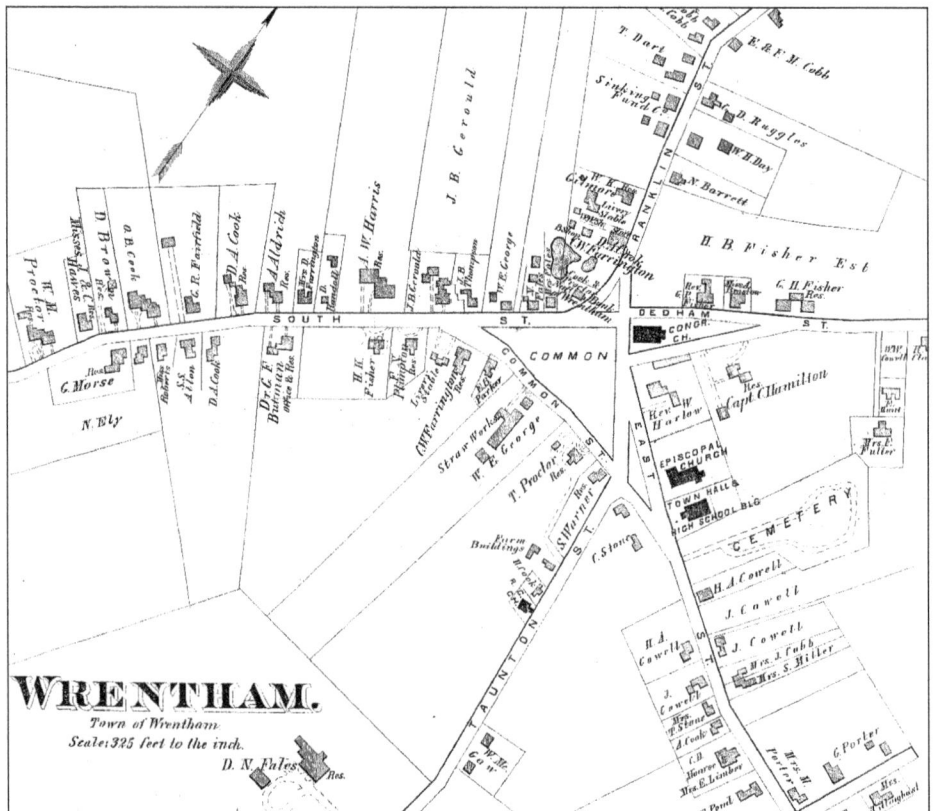

WRENTHAM.
Town of Wrentham
Scale: 325 feet to the inch.

INTRODUCTION

"At a General Court holden at Newe Towne, Sept. 2, 1635, it was ordered 'that there shall be a plantation settled about two miles above the Falls of Charles River on the northeast side thereof, to have ground lying to it on both sides of the river, both upland and meadow to be laid out hereafter as the Court shall appoint.'

On the 8th of September, 1636, the General Court ordered that the plantation to be settled above the Falls of Charles River shall have three years immunity from public charges, as Concord had, to be accounted from the first of May next, and the name of said plantation to be Dedham; to enjoy all that land on the southerly and easterly side of Charles River not formerly granted to any town or particular persons, and also to have five miles square on the other side of the river."

So begins Samuel Warner's *Historical Sketch of Wrentham*, published in 1880. According to Warner, as early as 1649 some inhabitants of Dedham went to Wallomonupoag, the area now known as Wrentham, to look for grass for their livestock. He quotes a record as follows: "Dedham 22, 4, 1660, at a meeting of the Selectmen there Lieut. Fisher, Serg't. Fuller, Richard Wheeler, Ensign Fisher are deputed to view the land, both upland and meadow near about the ponds by Indian George's wigwam, and make report of what they find to the Selectman on the first opportunity they can take."

It wasn't until a petition from the inhabitants of the new plantation was submitted to the Dedham Selectmen, and after Philip Sachem "sold" the natives' rights to the land, that the Dedham Selectmen allowed the plantation to become a town on October 17, 1673, and directed that its name should be Wrentham. It was a much larger town then. Remember that one requirement was that inhabitants should attend Sunday meetings; it was at those meetings that they held their religious services and attended to town affairs. The meetings, however, created a hardship for those living some distance from the meetinghouse. The inhabitants of Wrentham's western section requested a meetinghouse of their own, and in 1737 the General Court set them off as a separate parish. The inhabitants of the new West Precinct in the following years requested to become a town on their own and finally, on March 2, 1778, the town of Franklin was incorporated. Part of eastern Wrentham was set off to form the town of Foxborough on June 10, 1778, along with land from Walpole, Stoughton, and Sharon. Both Franklin and Foxborough got an industrial lead on Wrentham when railroads, having to skirt around Cedar Swamp, came to Franklin on May 18, 1849, and to Foxborough in 1867. Wrentham's first train didn't come through until December 1, 1890. Before that date, boats from the Sheldon

Boat Works were hauled to Boston by wagons; to make shipping easier, Bennett chair parts were shipped to Boston to be assembled, which probably accounts for so few Bennett chairs remaining in Wrentham.

In spite of the lack of the railroad through Wrentham before 1890, the Sheldon Boat Works started and flourished in Sheldonville after Col. Rhodes Sheldon came to the area in the early 1800s. Later, one of his salesmen, Mr. Nash, started the Nash Boat Company across the road from the Sheldon company on the same stream. Straw hats were manufactured on East Street, in the Sheldonville area, and in the "village," as the center of town was called. Straw hat manufacturing became a major industry when the George brothers started business in the village and with the development of modern machinery. The business was purchased by Brown and Cowell; when the building burned and Cowell left the business, Brown built a new building and continued operating into the 20th century. In 1933, after the straw hat business had faded, the building was struck by lightning and burned to the ground. Shortly after the railroad came to town, the jewelry factory on Kendrick Street was purchased by the Winter brothers, and in 1900 the Winter Brothers Company, manufacturers of taps and dies, was incorporated. It played a major role in providing war supplies during both world wars.

Formal education started in 1700 when the number of families in town exceeded 50. The number of schools grew, over time, to 19. Education beyond the primary grades was provided by private academies and, in Wrentham, the Day's Academy, whose charter is dated 1806. It continued to provide schooling to boys and girls until public high schools began, and when enrollment dropped to where the academy could no longer continue, the building was rented to the town of Wrentham to be used for their Center School.

In 1870, over 70 years after Reverend David Avery was dismissed from the Wrentham church and after he started a church in North Wrentham, that section of town was incorporated as the town of Norfolk. In 1905 Wrentham's Slacksville section separated and was incorporated as the town of Plainville, setting the borders of Wrentham to what they are today. Wrentham, once one of the larger towns south of Boston and in Suffolk County, became a much smaller town, and in 1793 was included in the newly formed county of Norfolk.

The 19th century saw considerable construction in Wrentham. In 1834 the Original Congregational Church was built in the "village," and only four years later, the Sheldonville Baptist Church was erected on West Street. Trinity Episcopal Church was built in 1872 at 47 East Street beside the Center School building, the replacement for the Day's Academy building, which had been moved to the east of the cemetery. The Center School burned to the ground in February 1895, and the Wrentham Public Library building was built on its foundation. A new Center School and town hall were built at the intersection of Dedham and Franklin Streets.

Following the arrival of the railroad in Wrentham in 1890 and electric street cars in 1902, the tourist industry grew by leaps and bounds. George's Park on Creek Street was taken over by William L. Enegren Jr., who had been operating a bakery on the grounds, and began its long history as Lake Pearl Park. The park had a dance hall, a beach and boat house, an outdoor theater, a picnic area, and an amusement park. Also on Lake Pearl, previously called Whiting's Pond, were three hotels for summer visitors. A street car siding came directly from the main line on Franklin Street into the park's automobile parking area.

The turn into the 20th century saw the straw hat business decline and the beginning of the Winter Brothers Company. From the time Winter Brothers started in 1900, it employed more and more local workers, expanding and contributing to the war production during both world wars.

One

WRENTHAM VILLAGE

The crossing of the road from Worcester to Taunton and the road from Dedham south to the Rhode Island line was the logical location for Wrentham's first meetinghouse. The village began and grew around a nucleus that remains the center today, even after so much of its original territory was separated to become Franklin, Norfolk, Plainville, part of Foxboro, Walpole, Bellingham, and Medway. It was the village that saw the railroad come in 1890 and the street car tracks in 1902, with the two lines meeting beside the common. The village has lost the railroad and street cars but is now marked by the prominent Original Congregational Church, built in 1834 at the intersection, as well as the village common, set aside in colonial days for common use and training the militia.

This view toward South Street from the town common, taken early one spring at the end of the 19th century, is dominated by massive elm trees lining the roads. From left to right, a milk delivery man, Daniel Farrington, and an Earle & Prew Express wagon gather around the new watering trough, a gift of Oliver Everett in 1894.

About 1895, while photography was still quite a novelty, this group lined up to be included as a photographer shot a view showing 40 South Street with an Earle & Prew's Express wagon in front. To the left is the entrance to the public library (up the stairs) and to the right, the railroad passenger station is visible in the distance.

Before the trolley lines were built along South Street in 1901, an early winter snow made for a beautiful winter scene. Standing in front of Cowell's building and looking south, the street is lined with maple and elm trees and has no overhead wires what-so-ever. The Gerould homestead (102 South Street) and the David Avery house (now 130 South Street) can be seen on the right.

At the end of the 19th century, a winter storm caused this scene in the center of Wrentham. With no street car tracks plowed through the snow, there appears only horse and sleigh tracks to upset what now looks like a picture postcard view of the town, although in actual fact, such storms greatly increased the hard work and discomfort to those who farmed the land.

With "the Italians laying the car tracks" in the background in April 1900, Frederick A. Shepard, who became tax collector for 1903–1904, walks towards the stores from the First National Bank of Wrentham. Note the carriage sheds behind the Congregational church and, on the left, the stairway leading to the police station under the bank.

Bank, Post Office and Town Hall, Wrentham, Mass.

The original bank building (pictured here) had two front doors to serve the two banks, the National Bank of Wrentham and the Wrentham Co-operative Bank, although at least for some of the time a single teller served both simply by moving to the appropriate window. The bank was also the Wrentham Post Office at the time of this photograph.

12

Looking northeast from in front of Francis' Store about 1905, one might see a street car at the stop on the common. Also visible are the carriage sheds behind the Congregational church, the band stand, and a group of boys playing ball on the common. Note the wooden barrel for storing rain water; town water was not yet available.

Large elm trees line Wrentham's streets in this early 1900s postcard photograph. A sign that reads "Womans Exchange" is hanging where the public library once rented space. George Francis operated the store on the near corner, and town water was now available, as was telephone service, electrical power, and street cars to Plainville and Franklin. The Foxborough line now came to the center, allowing people to transfer from one line to the other.

13

This building was built about 1840 and in 1917 housed Redding's Store. Standing in front in the above photo are Fred Redding and Morton Barnard. The photo below, taken inside, features a chocolate display for Valentine's Day, 1917. The posted warrant in the background announces the upcoming town meeting on March 5, a carry over from when March was the first month of the calendar year and expenditures and other town actions were voted on for the year ahead. This historic landmark was demolished in October 1971.

A glimpse down Kendrick Street at the end of the 19th century reveals a jewelry factory on the left, the new railroad passenger station at the end of the street, the house of Nathan Fales on the right, and before that the livery of Lewis Fisher. The Fisher stable and barn were later remodeled into a duplex dwelling where Eddie Larsen, one of Fisher's drivers, and the Larsen family ran a taxi service into the mid-20th century.

Looking up Kendrick Street from Fisher's Livery, one would have seen the rear of Samuel Cowell's house and Harrington's Lunch Cart, which burned on July 17, 1928. Harrington then moved across the street to what eventually became the Star Lunch.

The Winter Brothers Company, just down the street, provided many customers, who crowded the lunch cart as well as The Corner Shop and Davis' Store every workday at noon.

Few roads were paved in the 1920s, and many young men became interested in motorcycles since they cost less than an automobile. They were cheaper to operate, could travel over roads that would stop autos, and were exciting. In 1928, William Startz operated this motorcycle and bicycle shop at what is now 82 South Street.

From Daniel Farrington's front yard at 79 South Street, the Wrentham Post Office can be seen on the left, Pierce's Market is visible near the center, and to the right, one can just see the roof of a touring car as it starts down Kendrick Street toward the railroad station.

From the Congregational church steeple, a look to the south reveals Daniel Brown's house and carriage house on the left. To the right of that, Charles Brown's house is visible with the Wrentham Straw Works behind it. In the distance one can see the fields behind the Fales Farm on Taunton Street and Knuckup Hill, where two of Wrentham's water storage tanks now sit.

The first wet snowfall of the winter of 1902–1903 was the ideal time to capture this scene on a photographic plate. The tracks left by the first trolley car of the day are visible and the tree limbs are heavily laden, waiting for the sun to break through, causing the trees to sparkle until free of their extra load.

18

By 1934 the front doors of the bank building had been replaced by this single door with the name NATIONAL BANK OF WRENTHAM over it. "Cappie" Blaisdell's delivery truck is parked in front of the store and the gas pump remains in use. The new Route 1 is now finished, so this has been renamed Route 1A.

Government restrictions were not as confining in 1934 as they are today, as evidenced by this photograph showing a gasoline pump located beside the sidewalk and right outside of Francis' Store. One would swing an overhead pipe out over the sidewalk and "fill-up" from the attached hose. The sign indicates the price of a gallon of Socony gasoline was 12 1/2¢.

Casper T. Blaisdell (on the left), with his son-in-law, "Midge" Ross (to the rear), took over the Curtis Stone and Son grocery store in the Proctor Block and became the town clerk at the same time. The Blaisdell family continued to run the store long after World War II.

This 1941 photograph of 78–82 South Street shows the location of the Wrentham Post Office as well as Miller's Market, formerly Pierce's Market. At the right end of this photo is the South Street Diner.

Clinton B. "Doc" Davis bought the George Francis Store in 1939. He is shown here being introduced to Governor Bradford by Board of Selectmen Chairman Warren R. Gilmore, who later served the town as postmaster.

"Doc" Davis's wife, Goldie, and teenager Tommy Donaldson work behind the ice cream and sandwich counter in this World War II–era photograph.

Bradford Harrison, the son-in-law of Doc and Goldie, worked at and later ran the store as a family business. Here he is at the newspaper counter at the rear of the store selling a paper to Fred Brown.

Keeping the business family oriented, Brad employed his father, shown here arranging the shelves, along with Joy Ross and Sandra Jenkins.

Two

OUR TWO LARGE LAKES

It was a search by early settlers from Dedham for new grass that led them to ". . . view the land, both upland and meadow, near about the ponds by George Indians' wigwam . . ." Those ponds, later known as Blake's Pond and Whiting's Pond, are now known as Lake Archer and Lake Pearl. It was George's Park (renamed Lake Pearl Park when purchased by William Enegren in 1891) on the shore of Whiting's Pond that attracted the lake tourists to what became Lake Pearl. With the coming of the electric street railroad in 1902 to Lake Archer, summer cottages were added every year, and by World War II they dotted almost the whole shoreline of both lakes. About a half dozen on each lake were year-round residences.

Less than a mile north of the village, the area known as Marsh Pond, now Mirror Lake, was dammed to raise the water level. Several years after World War I it, too, began to see the building of summer cottages.

Wrentham, with its two wonderful lakes, has been a popular playground of eastern Massachusetts and northern Rhode Island beginning in the late 1800s with George's Park and moving well into the 1900s. That Wrentham could accommodate the large incoming crowds is evidenced by this view showing the Lake Pearl Hotel on the right, Weinstein's Hotel just right of the center, and the boathouse and beach facilities of the park. Also visible on the left is an ice house where ice, after being cut on the lake each winter, was hauled up the slide and stored to provide for the making of ice cream at the park.

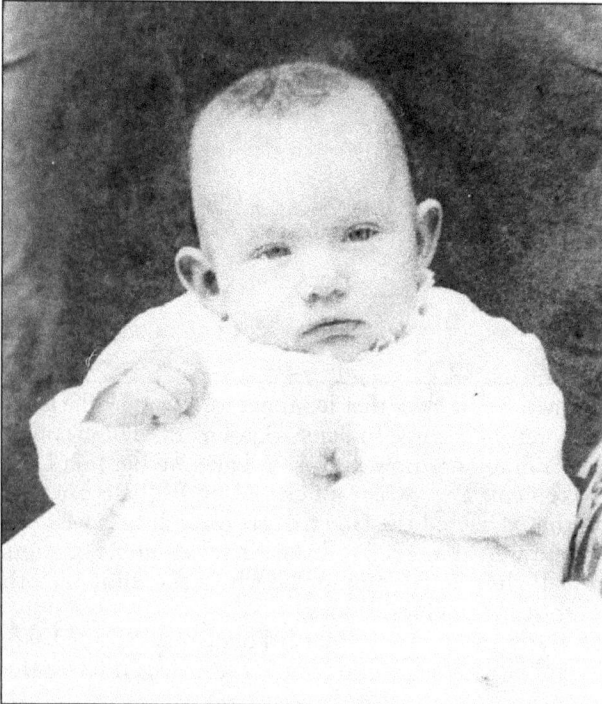

Pearl Lillian Enegren was born on July 25, 1887, and died four months later. William L. Enegren Jr., after he bought George's Park in 1891, renamed it Lake Pearl Park in memory of his daughter and Whiting's Pond soon became known as Lake Pearl. The 40-foot-long excursion boat *Pearl of the Lake* was built and launched in 1909.

Weinstein's Lake Pearl Manor was devastated by fire in June of 1927, just before the beginning of the tourist season, shutting the hostelry down until it was rebuilt. The New Weinstein's, below, opened the next year and flourished well into the 1940s. The property was sold and the hotel demolished on August 6, 1970.

WEINSTEIN'S LAKE PEARL MANOR, WRENTHAM, MASSACHUSETTS

Also along the easterly shore of Lake Pearl was the Hotel Lake Pearl, later renamed The Woodcock Inn. It was destroyed by fire on December 9, 1931.

The least well known of the three hotels on Lake Pearl, and the one that existed for the shortest time before being destroyed by fire, was the Washington Park Hotel, located on the hill above the other two hotels, both of which were on the waterfront.

In 1909, the attraction to Lake Pearl Park was so great that special trolley cars ran to it, and the open cars used in the summer made for a very pleasant trip. The special track, running from the bottom of Eagle Hill, brought riders directly into the park through the "upper" entrance near the dance hall, the concession stands, the merry-go-round, and the outdoor theater. The beach and boat landing were only a short stroll down the hill.

The great popularity of Lake Pearl Park caused the MA&W Electric Street Railway to lay tracks from the bottom of Eagle Hill, where the road bed is still clearly visible, right into the park.

The "lower" entrance to Lake Pearl Park was the auto entrance in the early 1900s, while the "upper" entrance was where the trolley track led to the parking lot. It was a busy time for the park, and on any bright summer weekend, two police officers were required to be on duty at the entrance alone.

Even before noon on this fine summer's day in 1919, the "Auto Park" at Lake Pearl Park was starting to fill up. People came by autos, trains, electric street cars, bicycles, and by foot to enjoy a day at the beach, boating, band concerts, an outdoor theater, and the amusement park.

This September 17, 1916 photograph of the boat landing and beach at Lake Pearl Park is a sure indication that, unless one were actually swimming, the correct dress of the day for ladies was long dresses, a jacket, and a bonnet; for gentlemen, it was a suit, tie, and straw hat.

The higher level of the park area provided a grand view of the lake, and guests would often spend hours watching the canoes, rowboats, and sailboats that dotted the lake. The *Pearl of the Lake* was also a common sight on the lake.

William L. Enegren Jr. ran a bakery in Franklin with Mr. Arnold, and started a bakery at George's Park on Whiting's Pond in Wrentham. He bought the park from Lyman George's widow in 1891. After the death of his daughter Pearl, the pond and park were renamed Lake Pearl and Lake Pearl Park. His efforts led to one of the premium tourists attractions in the Northeast, accommodating many company outings and dances that saw all the big bands of the 1930s and early '40s, until World War II curtailed the gasoline necessary to allow patrons to drive to the park. The downturn of the big bands after the war caused the park to change its style of operation.

On a fine Sunday afternoon in 1910, Lake Pearl Park, with all its concession stands open, is crowded with ladies in their best "go to meeting" outfits (including straw bonnets) and men in suits, often with straw hats. The park, by now, had earned a fine reputation as one of the best in the Northeast.

World War 1 ended almost a year previous to this photograph being taken and people once again began to relax at the park. The regular band concerts even attracted some boaters from the lake on this Sunday, August 3, 1919.

The natural topography at Lake Pearl Park lent itself to an outdoor theater with a stage backing up to the lake. Theater-goers could watch the shows, or if the show was not good, watch the activities on the lake. It must have been a challenge to the performers to draw patrons' attention away from the *Pearl* sailing by or from the "courting" going on in the canoes in the background.

Each year late in the spring curious onlookers from the park and from around the lake watched the *Pearl* get launched from her winter dry dock.

On the bright Sunday afternoon of September 17, 1916, the motor launch *Pearl*, full to capacity, made one of her many trips around the lake, much to the delight of her passengers.

World War I was nearing an end when this patriotic theme of American flags and red, white, and blue streamers was used to decorate the Lake Pearl Ballroom in 1917.

An early photograph, taken looking onto Creek Street from the front yard of the George home on South Street, shows still unpaved roads, but the barely discernible signs say "Lake Pearl Auto Club Inn," "Chicken-Steak Dinners," and "Open the Year Around."

In this photograph, taken from Red Dam looking toward Eagle Dam and Franklin Street, the old Whiting house is on the left and 656 Franklin Street is in the center. The Whiting house was destroyed long ago.

Looking east, the house at 668 Franklin Street sits on the hill to the left; in the left foreground is a small roadside stand. The pole just to the left of the center indicates that electric power, other than that provided for the street cars, had come to Wrentham. Electric car tracks of the MA&W Street Railway run along the right, and beyond the pine tree is 656 Franklin Street.

A spring in the cove at the easterly end of Lake Pearl was a very convenient location to set up a soda bottling works. Over the years it went by many names other than the Indian Red Spring, which is what it was called at the time of this photograph.

Looking northwest from what is now Oak Point in the very late 1800s, the only building visible is the Red Farm, the summer home of Edgar Chamberlain, correspondent for *The Boston Transcript*. Helen Keller was a summer guest there from 1894 until she moved to Wrentham in 1905.

On September 6, 1909, Wrentham Day, featuring swimming and boating contests, took place at the north end of Lake Archer. The introduction of the trolley line running along Franklin Street in 1902 brought construction to the shore, which 10 years earlier had been nothing but empty beaches. Building along Franklin Street also flourished in that period, as can be seen in this photo.

By the end of the summer of 1914, cottages were built all along the shores of Lake Archer, as evidenced in this view taken from Franklin Street. The Labor Day festivities had, by then, become an annual event, and brought out, in addition to the boats, flags, and swimmers, a photographer to capture it on a 5-by-8-inch glass plate. The car parked on the shore looks like a 1909 Rambler.

At the 1914 Wrentham celebration on Lake Archer, Charles C. Winter (second from the left) won three medals for water-related activities. He is shown here with his three companions after they won a boating contest.

Before the proliferation of summer cottages, Carl Snyder's Sandy Beach at the end of Archer Street was the favorite swimming place for those living along Archer Street and most of the kids living between the town's center and "Peanut" corner.

This pre-1900 photograph was taken from Franklin Street in front of the Red Farm looking out over Lake Archer. Note that there are no buildings along the shore and that the area known now as Oak Point is quite bare, enough so that the Council Oak towers above the surrounding area.

This photograph was taken several years after the one on the bottom of the previous page, looking easterly along the southern shore of Lake Archer. On the right is the ice house of W.A. McGaw of Taunton Street.

Three

THE WEST END OF TOWN

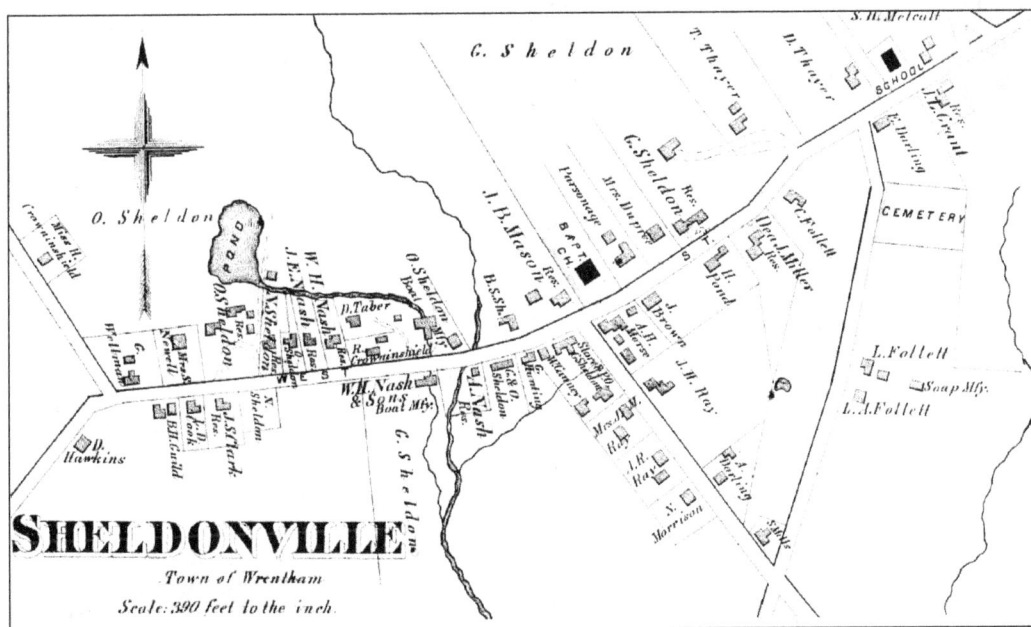

The west end of Wrentham was primarily farming country until Col. Rhodes Sheldon arrived from Cumberland and started building boats. Craftsmen started to settle around the boat shop and this second concentration of residents soon became known as Sheldonville. The area grew to include a blacksmith shop, a general store, a post office, schools, a church, a cemetery, a gristmill, a lumber mill, and a second boat shop. In West Wrentham, a second post office was established, along with a private school, water-powered mills, a blacksmith shop, a cemetery, and a church. The area even boasted a gold mine, although it was never rich enough to last long or to make any money.

Col. Rhodes Sheldon came to the west end of Wrentham in 1823 and soon started building boats. The availability of excellent boat-building materials along with his increased expertise prompted him to start the Sheldon Boat Works, which he located on the north side of West Street, along the stream. He sold boats locally and then started carting them to Boston for sale.

George Sheldon, the son of Rhodes, along with others in the Sheldon family carried on the Sheldon Boat Works after the death of its founder. The Sheldons hired a number of craftsmen at the boat works and built housing for some of them along West and Hancock Streets.

The "Long House," 1085–91 West Street, was built as a boardinghouse for boat factory workers from the Sheldon Boat Works shop, which was located across the street. It probably also housed some workers from Alfred Nash's boat shop, located downstream from Sheldon's and on the south side of West Street, as noted by the sign in this early photograph.

Alfred Nash, once a salesman for the Sheldon Boat Works, eventually started building boats himself. A smaller operation, less well known than Sheldon's, the Nash boats appear, from this photograph, to be just as well built and just as beautiful.

Looking east on West Street one can see the Baptist church on the left, the parsonage next to it, and the Sheldonville Store on the right edge of the photo.

The Sheldonville Store was operated *c.* 1900 by E. Scott. The sign in the center reads "WANTED, To Buy Farm Produce of All Kinds, such as Butter, Eggs, Poultry and Vegetables of all kinds."

This postcard photograph of the J.T. Hutchinson Jr. General Store has the note "This was taken at 3 P.M. April 22, 1914. 8 hours later it was burned to the ground."

Several houses along Hancock Street, just south of West Street, were built by the Sheldons to provide housing for the boat workers. Some workers were allowed to direct part of their wages toward owning the houses, which helped both the workers and the Sheldons.

Next to the minister and the miller, a blacksmith was probably the most important man in the village. To encourage a blacksmith to serve the town, it voted in 1687 to allot 10 acres of land at the corner of Dedham and East Streets to encourage the settlement of blacksmith Samuel Dearing. Pictured above is a Sheldonville blacksmith shop; Nelson Falk is busy at his forge in the photograph below. Blacksmiths performed a most important community function—fabricating and maintaining farm, industrial, and home equipment.

Looking east, the stonewall on the left is in front of Judge Samuel Day's house at 996 West Street. To the right is the first home of Asa Aldrich; in 1859 it belonged to Charles Follett, a boat builder.

This photograph appears to have been taken from the field in back of the Sheldonville Fire Station looking toward 1138–1170 West Street.

This country view is West Street going east and just approaching Cherry Street. Through the trees can be seen 760 West, the home of Amorous Follett and, later, his son Alonzo.

West Street in the area of houses numbered in the mid-1000s was a wide, elm-lined, well-traveled roadway with two boat-building manufacturers, a blacksmith, a store, and a post office close by.

The Sheldonville area was primarily a farming community in 1929, when this building served as Station 2 of the fire department. The town saw the need for an upgrade, and as can be seen by the station just 3 years later, it was voted to build a new one to house the new truck.

In 1932, the Wrentham Fire Department sported this new Combination truck housed at the Sheldonville Station on West Street. The distance of the west end of Wrentham from the main station meant that this truck got a lot of use. It was usually the first on the scene of fires in Sheldonville and West Wrentham.

Grant's Mill, located across from 1442 West Street, was owned by George Grant in 1851 and in 1888 by C.A. Grant. It produced lumber, shingles, and clapboards.

George Hettinger operated this gold mine. He had the ore assayed and sold stock but the ore was of such poor grade that the mine soon folded.

RFD mail delivery in the area of West Wrentham was assured by this solid means of transportation that could not be stopped by "rain, sleet, or snow." A determined mailman and his trusty steed posed for the cameraman in front of the West Wrentham Post Office on Ray Road in this late 1800s photo.

The West Wrentham Post Office was on West Street in this photo but West Street has since been re-routed and now its location is Ray Road. A part of that building remains at 15 Ray Road.

The Sheldonville Baptist Church was built in 1838 on West Street across from Hancock Street, and in 1839 the parsonage was built next to it. Note the clothes hanging on the line, and next to it, the home of Mortimer and Lillian Johnson.

The Baptist church, started by the Rev. Williams and sold to the Universalists in the early 1800s, was at the intersection of West and Williams Street and overlooked the West Wrentham Cemetery.

Four

How We Earned Our Keep

Early Wrentham was primarily a farming town and got a late start at industry, probably because it had no navigable rivers and the railroad didn't come through the village until 1890. Sheldon boats were shipped to Boston by wagon and team, as were Bennett chair parts, which were assembled there because that made shipping easier. Straw hats and jewelry were easier to transport. Franklin, Norfolk, and Foxboro had railroads years earlier and Walpole had also substantial water power with which to power machinery. The people of Wrentham did, however, survive, and earned their livings in a number of ways.

In 1913, 23-year-old Alfred George delivered provisions for the William H. Pierce Market at 78 South Street. Several generations of the George family lived in Wrentham at 277 South Street from 1856 to 1969. Alfred's passenger is 5-year-old Dorothy Pierce.

William H. Pierce was a meat cutter and owned a meat and grocery market on South Street for many years.

Ben Willard worked as a meat cutter at Pierce's Market on South Street in the early 1900s and later started a slaughter house on the Willard property at the corner of Winter and Dedham Streets. Note the photographer's reflection in the glass behind Ben.

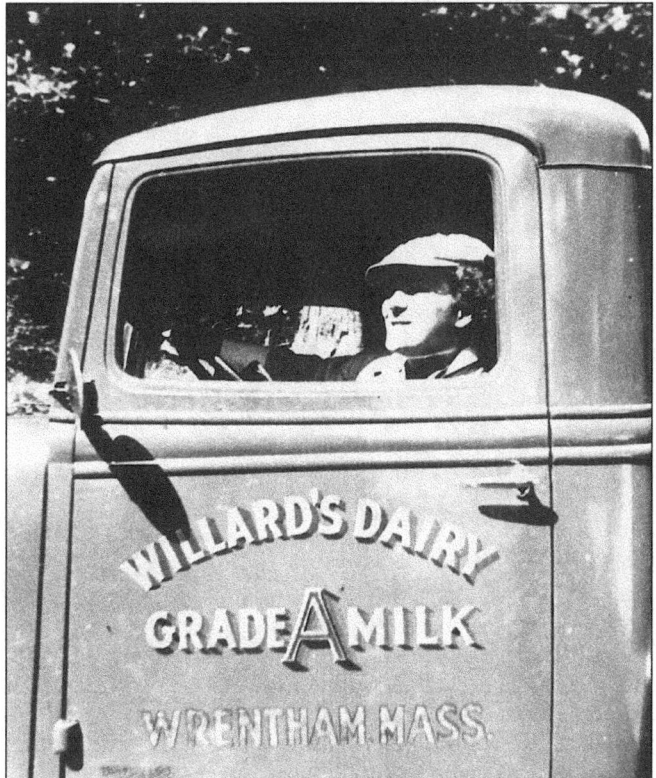

Ben Willard also ran a milk delivery business from his home on Winter Street. There were several local dairies and milk delivery companies in town including Wrentham Dairy, Whipple's, Cartier's, and Hatt's. Some had dairy herds and others bought their milk.

Sam Shanker started his shoe repair shop next to Blaisdell's Market (previously Stone and Son) in what was an addition to the Procter Block. Sam later moved to a larger place next to the A&P in the next building.

Daniel Cook's general merchandise store, located on the first floor of Cook's Hall, was later joined in the building by Thomas' store. Being situated directly across from the new Center School assured vigorous candy sales.

CURTIS, STONE & SON,

—DEALERS IN—

CHOICE FAMILY GROCERIES
AND GENERAL MERCHANDISE,

Such as Hardware, Wooden Ware, Crockery and Glass Ware, Farming Tools, Patent Medicines, Drugs, &c. Men's Rubber Boots and Shoes, Leather Gloves and Mittens. High grades of Tea and Coffee a specialty. Home Made Bread Fresh every Morning.

ALL GOODS WARRANTED AS REPRESENTED.
WRENTHAM CENTRE.

This ad appeared in the 1890 Wrentham and Norfolk Directory.

Mrs. Stone of the Curtis Stone and Sons Store in the Procter Block visits with an unidentified clerk in this early 1900s photograph. Note that, although the store was equipped with electric lights, the uncertainty of electric power necessitated the retention of a hanging kerosene lamp, "just in case."

The job of feeding the thousands of ducks when they were outside consisted of shoveling feed from the back of a moving truck. Inside the long buildings, feed was moved in wheeled hand trucks running on steel tracks, much like coal being taken out of mines.

The opening of the Weber Duck Inn on the new "State Road" (now Route1A but at that time Route 1) on April 19, 1923, marked the beginning of what was to become one of the best-known road houses in the Northeast. David Weber and his brother John teamed up with Leon Pini, a chef at the Woodcock Cafe in Boston, to accommodate thousands of customers every April to November (New England roads were often impassable in winter) until 1934, when Leon Pini departed to start running the Lafayette House in Foxborough. Business declined steadily until 1942, when the National Bank of Wrentham started foreclosure proceedings against the company.

The Weber Duck Inn and farm had a small roadside store along Dedham Street where they sold dressed Pekin ducks and 13 oz. cans of Duck Giblet Gravy.

This is the small store, located 200 yards north of the Weber Duck Inn on the same side of the Boston to Providence Highway, where the dressed ducks and cans of duck gravy were sold to the motoring public.

The large building in front was likely the former Moses Whitney Tavern, but by the time this photograph was taken, it had become a rooming house for employees of the George Brother's straw hat factory, visible in the rear.

This photo, taken with no artificial light, required everyone in the picture to stay very still because photographic plates were so slow and exposure time was so long. Note the hat forms, which were usually made of wood or plaster, that were used to form the wet straw.

The Eagle Mill, also called the Eagle Manufacturing Company, was located between Franklin Street and Eagle Dam. All that remains is part of the rear foundation wall, now serving as a low retaining wall. The Whiting home can be seen at the right rear.

The Eagle Manufacturing Company was located on the "Worchester to Taunton" Road (Franklin Street). It was an impressive brick building, although its existence was relatively short. The house visible to the left is now 588 Franklin Street.

In 1901, less than a year after its incorporation, Winter Brothers Company workers gathered at the Kendrick Street entrance of what had been the jewelry factory for this group photograph. They are, from left to right, as follows: (front row) Jack Leonard, Bob Redding, Dick Barton, Charlie "Toot" Bishop, Sidney Hall, Frank Shepard, and Spike Shaunessy; (back row) Nat Grant, Murray Winter, Harry Bennett, Fred Sheppard, and George Barnes.

It was not many years later that the Winter Brothers Company had to expand the plant to include the brick addition shown here.

Factory workers at the Winter Brother's Company stopped for this photo in 1939. Included are Tom Fox, Edgar Redding, Martin Spaulding, Owen Newcombe, James Fitzgerald Sr., Benjamin Grover, Harold Waite, Frank Quirk, Fred Grant, "Bowser" Malloy, Leroy Jenness Sr., James Daley, A. Whitman Jamieson, Albert K. Locklin, John Colletto Sr., Sigurd Larsen, John Knapp, Magnus Larsen, and Chester Willard.

In 1929, the Winter Brother's office sported the latest office machines and even boasted its own switchboard with Lounette Roby, fresh out of school, as the operator.

Warren K. and Ellen Gilmore's 50th wedding anniversary was the occasion for this photograph, which gathered together sons Fred E., Charles A., Frank R., and George W., all of whom were engaged in various capacities running the W.K. Gilmore and Sons business. The company, suppliers of coal, grain, and associated products, started in Norfolk and Wrentham in 1876, and added Walpole in 1890, Franklin in 1912, Medfield in 1928, and Canton in 1931.

W.K. Gilmore's coal sheds were located along the main railroad line at the end of Depot Street. After being extensively damaged by fire on Feb. 8, 1946, and with the increasing reliance on oil heat, the sheds were demolished.

Before refrigeration, ice was cut from ponds and saved for use in the warm months of summer. The Providence Ice Company had a large facility on the eastern shore of Lake Archer. When the ice was thick enough, the company hired many workers to cut ice, which was then pulled up a motorized conveyor to be stored for later use, or to be loaded onto railroad cars parked on the special siding (below) and hauled to the city.

MAIN DINING ROOM

UPPER DECK

THE WRENTHAM SHOW BOAT. INC.. WRENTHAM. MASS. ON ROUTE NO. 1 BOSTON TO PROVIDENCE ROAD

When Route 1 was new, this restaurant and lounge was built near the end of Madison Street. It was built and decorated like a ship and was named, appropriately, the Show Boat.

Jansen's 1934 Dodge was parked at the gas pumps at the Sheldonville Store and Post Office on a winter's day in 1935. A.L. Page was the store proprietor at this time as well as a volunteer firefighter at the Sheldonville Station. The Jansens operated a greenhouse at the corner of West and Cherry Streets, raising flowers that they regularly transported to Boston.

Hagopian's Red Bird Farm, started in 1910 on Taunton and Beach Streets by blind George Hagopian, was one of the largest hen farms in New England. He raised thousands of Rhode Island Red chicks every year in several large three-story hen houses and shipped them, often by U.S. Mail, to all parts of the country. In October 1949, one of those houses along Taunton Street burned, killing thousands of chickens. The business never fully recovered from the loss and is no longer operating.

The Wrenmere Inn was located where the Fales Farm sat off Taunton Street. After the large section burned, the two sections on the left were moved by George Mayshaw to 69 Taunton Street, right beside his house at 61 Taunton Street. The remainder of the inn was torn down in November 1935 to make room for the construction of the George L. Vogel School. Pictured below is the "Sun Parlor," which is now the rear section of the home at 69 Taunton Street.

Sun Parlor. Wrenmere
Wrentham, Mass.

Bishop's Tavern at 513 South Street became a very popular road house. It was located on what was then Route 1, the main coastal highway from Maine to Florida, and was a favorite meeting place for many going to and from the Narragansett Race Track. At the end of World War II, servicemen returning to Wrentham often gathered at the Hunter's Bar in the basement to swap war stories.

Among those in this post–World War II photograph of the Hunter's Bar are John Colletto, Robert Nelson, Frank McGarry, Tony Nardelli, William Palmer, Edward O'Connor, Walter George, and George Clentimack.

Nathan Webber, at 45 Dedham Street, ran this ad in the 1890 Wrentham and Norfolk Directory. He ran the business until he was killed at a railroad crossing in Attleboro.

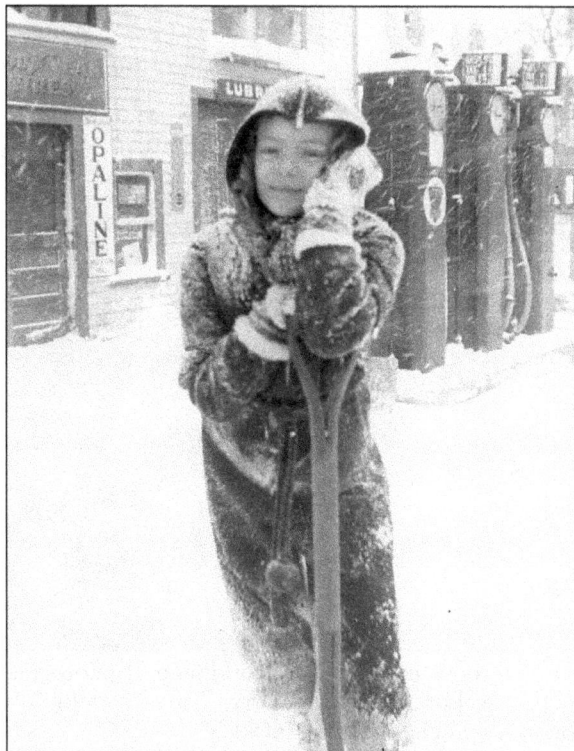

Frank Dunlap, the town clerk from 1929 until his death in 1944, also ran this filling station and garage at 45 Dedham Street. His granddaughter, Laura Lou Startz, sometimes helped by shoveling snow from around the gas pumps.

At the end of each school day, Donald Ross would hurry to work at the busy Cliffdale filling station, located near the Plainville town line on what was then U.S. Route 1, the Coastal Highway.

Walter H. Stewart was the foreman of the Winter Brothers Company threading department for almost 46 years. He also operated an insurance agency and was a longtime fireman and water commissioner.

Dot Ames ran this dry goods store and, in the rear, a hairdressing shop. She was located between two grocery stores, the IGA store of Al Schwalbe and the A&P store.

The original dry goods store was severely damaged in a fire. After it was rebuilt, but before it was owned by Dot Ames, it was run by Earl MacCabe.

On the morning after the fire, Louis H. Roby's team and wagon are backed up to the building that housed the dry goods store.

Pierce's Market on South Street was bought by Walter Miller. Lined up in front of the rationed goods display are Frank Kirstein, Charles Moore, Walter Miller, Arthur "Yarda" Riley, and Hiram Bly.

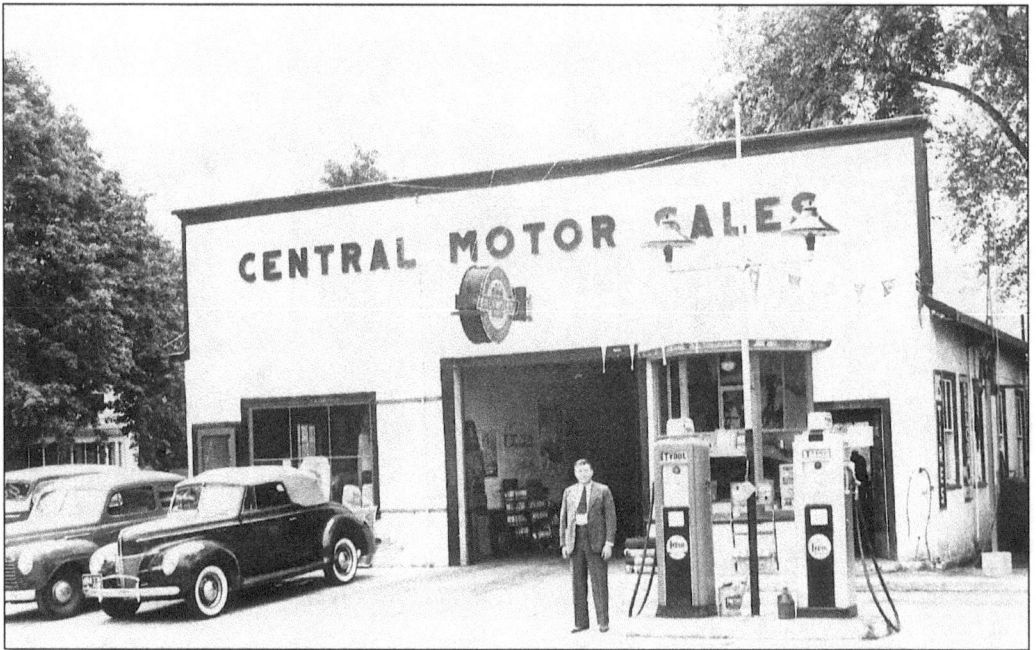

Leo Lavallee, standing by the gas pumps, first worked as a mechanic for Alec's Garage at 15 Common Street. He eventually bought the business and the Chevrolet dealership, and called it Central Motor's Sales.

Salesmen are ready to introduce the new 1937 Chevrolets. The gentleman on the right is Warren Gilmore.

From the air, this photo of the Crosby-Ashton plant, previously owned by the Winter Bros., shows its location near the railroad tracks. At the top of the photo one can see the railroad freight station, the burned remains of W.K. Gilmore's coal sheds, and Gilmore's grain storage building.

The Crosby Valve and Gage Company, a pioneer in the development of large nuclear valves, displays an exceptionally large one. The sign reads "Nuclear Turbine Valve—supplied to Westinghouse for installation in Taiwan."

During the 1919 Welcome Home celebration, the bank, along with most other buildings in the village, was appropriately decorated. The George W. MacInnis American Legion Post #225 had a meeting place in the bank building.

Cook's Hall at one time served as a greeting card assembly business. This group has gathered for a Christmas party.

Five

SOME OCCASIONAL IMAGES

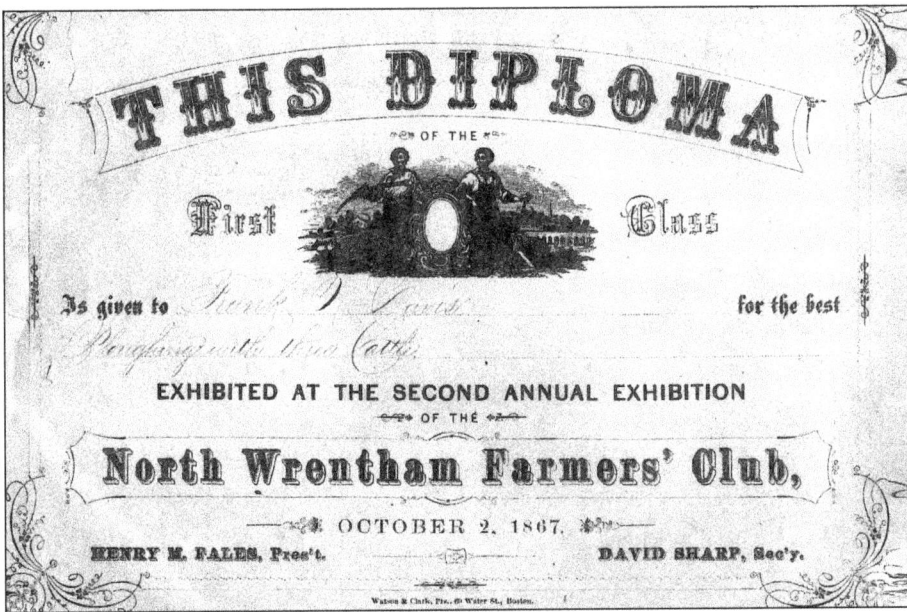

When something unusual or significant happens, there are often people around to preserve the occasion for future viewing. Not all happenings were photographed, and many of those that were are no longer still available. Many important pictures have been lost since the birth of photography. The following pictures will at least get a little more exposure and be around longer because they have made it into print.

Taking pictures using wet glass plates and large cameras was a laborious process made a bit easier when dry plates came along, and even easier when flexible film was developed. Because of the painstaking nature of early photography, it is reasonable to conclude that the subjects of early photographs were very important to somebody.

Wrentham's GAR hall was on South Street in the Slacksville section of town, now Plainville. Members lined up, along with the Wrentham Brass Band, for the photograph above. The building burned to the ground on December 26, 1905.

Civil War veterans gathered, in uniform, on Wrentham Common for the dedication of its second Civil War monument in 1915. An earlier monument was placed in the Plainville section of town when it was still Wrentham, but when Plainville was incorporated in 1905, Wrentham was left with no monument.

In 1924, veterans, friends, and guests gathered for the dedication of the World War I Flag Pole Memorial, designed by local artist and veteran Joseph G. Cowell.

One of the many activities for Wrentham's 250th anniversary was this group of young dancers, shown here rehearsing on East Street, opposite the common. Standing on the right are Earle Stewart and William Pierce, sitting is Joseph Sylvia, and standing on the left is Margaret Overleas. The girl on the extreme left remains unidentified.

From 1859 the Roman Catholic Church used the lower floor of this building at 54 Taunton Street as its chapel. It was operated first as a Boston Mission and later as a mission of the Foxborough church until a new building was built at 140 South Street in 1928. This photograph was taken in 1925, probably after Easter Mass.

Mr. William Sweatt's will of 1926 stated that his home at 289 East Street (see p. 106) would go to the King's Daughters and Sons. He died in Italy in 1929, the result of a fall. When his wife died, the property was transferred and it was dedicated as the Pond Home on January 20, 1934, replacing the home on Valley Street in Norfolk.

When the Blake Brother's buildings at 343 and 349 East Street were the Jordan Marsh Rest Home for employees, the back fields were used for many community functions. A St. Mary's Church picnic was the occasion for this group of young ladies to gather for a photographer. They are, from left to right, as follows: (seated) Marilyn Mitchell, Jean Cooney, Jean Buckley, Fran Jordan, and Joan Cooney; (standing) Loretta Colletto, Betty Mitchell, Dotty Lockwood, Alma Jordan, Dotty Lavallee, and ? Lund.

The installation committee included the following, from left to right: (front row) Howard Parker, John Crowley, and Frederick Heffron; (back row) Earle Swett, Joseph Riley, Elliott MacDowell, and Thurman Andrew.

On May 30, 1937, these members of the George W. MacInnis American Legion Post #225 gathered on the front lawn at 135 South Street before the Memorial Day parade. They are, from left to right, as follows: (front row) Earle Swett, Joseph Cowell, Richard VanUmmerson, Bert Shepard, Patrick Dolan, Joseph Lyman, Thomas Aylward, Walter Duffy, Wesley Hamilton, and Guy Stevens; (back row) John A. Warren, Fred Heffron, Russell Thompson, Thomas Proctor, Howard Parker, "Harry" Passey, Warren Gilmore, Henry Knox, Ernest Munroe, Robert McClain, Elmer Young, Edward Smith, and Joseph Riley.

In 1944, as part of the war effort, the Lion's Club of Wrentham conducted a waste paper drive. In this group, lined up in front of Leo Lavallee's Central Motor Sales, are Chief Charles Bishop, Elmer Snow, Buster Willard, Gus Scott, Earle Sanford, Warren Gilmore, Jack Randall, Carlin "Chick" Nightingale, Walter Duffy, Charles McDougald, Frank Kirstein, Paul "Rig" Giannetti, Charles and Harriett Rice, Leo Lavallee, Frank Kerrissey, and Milt Webber. The children include Al Hooper, Al Fuller, and a number of others not yet identified.

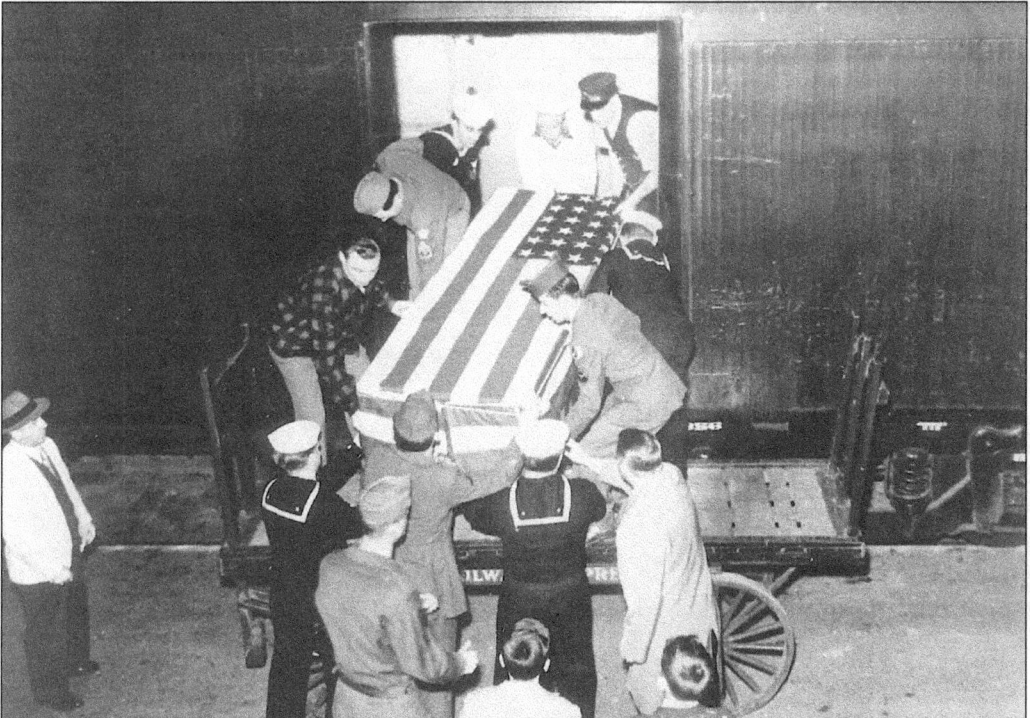

At 5:04 p.m. on Monday, November 1, 1948, the body of Lt. Kenneth Ames was returned from France and was unloaded at the Franklin Railroad Station by some of his schoolmates, including Henry, John, and Gus Colletto.

On December 2, 1954, these Wrentham telephone operators were on hand for this last photo of the switchboard in operation, for this was the day that Wrentham switched to the dial system. The town switchboard was located in the rear of the small house located just below 24 Kendrick Street. From left to right are Velma Perry, Charlotte Hatch, Ada Haehnel, Dotty Larsen, Grace Gleichauf, Yvette Cook, and Geneva Gilpatrick. Missing from the photo, having worked the night shift, are Ruth Ellis and Hilda Wyllie.

On December 2, 1954, Wrentham was switched over to the telephone dial system. Selectmen Earle Stewart and Earl Harris watch Chairman Arthur Gleichauf making a phone call as a phone company official looks on.

It must have been a long trip for the postman to deliver mail to the one house on Everett Street in Wrentham, and one wonders if the mail was delivered daily when the weather wasn't as pleasant as it was early in the 1900s when this photo was taken.

When the new Maxim Chemical Fire Truck arrived in 1920, Stan Chilson was there to photograph it with, from left to right, Joseph P. Quirk, Daniel S. Farrington, Wesley G. Dibblee, Chief George H. E. Mayshaw, and driver Theodore Swenson.

In the photograph, handwritten labels read:

Eic Bliek — Capt. Jenkens — Capt. Coyle — Knapp — Chief Coyle — McLean — Leit Williams — Miller — Leit. Riley — Quirk — Hurd — George

Comb. No.2. — Pump — Comb. No.1. — Ladder No.1. — Forest Fire Service

WRENTHAM FIRE DEPT.
MAY 30, 1931

For Memorial Day, 1931, Wrentham's fire apparatus was lined up in front of the Central Station, located behind the "new" Center School at Franklin and Dedham Street. Pictured are Engineer Jacob Bliek, Captain Clifford P. Jenkins Sr., Captain John Coyle, John Knapp, Fire Chief Thomas Coyle, Daniel MacLean, Lt. Mansfield Williams, Arthur Miller, Lt. Arthur Riley, Frank Quirk, Franklin Hurd, and Walter "Dutchy" George.

Chief Perley Dexter and Patrolman Charles Bishop stand proudly beside the brand new Oldsmobile patrol car in 1936. The brick building in the background is the First National Bank of Wrentham. The police station was downstairs; access was gained by an outdoor stairway on the left of the building.

Six

Schools
and Students

Any town with at least 50 families in the late 1600s was required to run a grammar school to teach children to ". . . read English and wright and cypher . . ." It seems we had 50 families in the late 1600s, but the selectmen avoided providing school until forced to do so "as the law direct." At a town meeting on December 19, 1701, the town took action to establish a school but no teacher could be found, so the selectmen, along with other townfolk, took turns teaching for a week at a time. In 1702, the town voted to build a school building "twenty foot long and sixteen foot broad," and in December of 1703 the services of Theodore Man were obtained to teach, starting the following January.

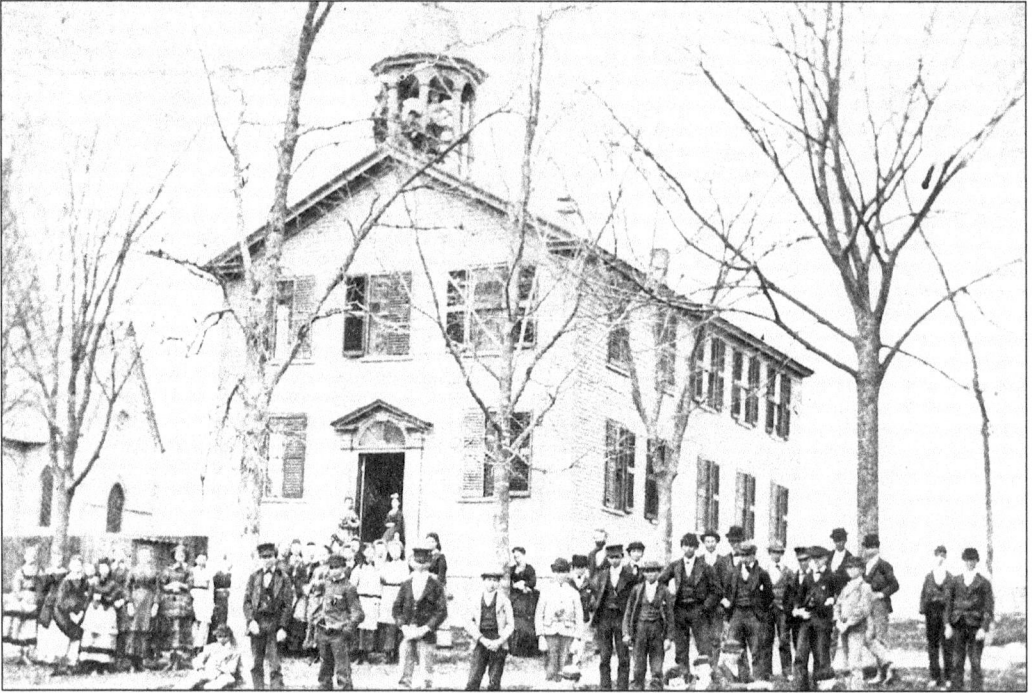

The General Court granted a charter in 1806 for a private institution, which was to become Day's Academy. It was located on the lower common until 1828, when it was moved to the hill at 55 East Street, the site now occupied by the first Fiske Public Library. Young men and women were educated here until about 1867, when Wrentham's first public high school was established.

When the Day's Academy building, rented by the town for a public school, was no longer suitable for school use, it was moved to the east side of the cemetery and this impressive building was built at its vacated location. Called the Centre School, it stood until it burned to the ground on February 21–22, 1895.

The Sheldonville School housed the first six grades of students living in the west end of town and was taught for many years by Nina Sheldon. From grades seven on, students were transported to the Center School, first by horse-drawn wagons and pungs, and in 1921 by motorized buses.

The first through fourth grades of the Sheldonville School lined up for a photograph in 1932. The students are, from left to right, as follows: (front row) Wood, Esau, Sprague, Cook, unknown, Moriarty, Meservie, Wheeler, and unknown: (middle row) Hatt, Cartier, Lippherdt, unknown, Wheeler, Wade, Turner, and Cook; (back row) Moriarty, Cartier, Cook, Grover, Grover, Curtis, Ordway, and Moriarty.

These pupils from the Wampum School *c.* 1888 have been identified, from left to right, as follows: (front row) Emma Martin, Walter Hatch, Dwight Heaton, Grace Bennett, Alice Draper, Fanny Fisher, Florence Bennett, Bill Draper, and Arthur Martin; (middle row) Olive Farnum, Laura Brown, Bert Bennett, and Lula Henry; (back row) Ella Thomas, Grace Wilmot, teacher Miss Mary A. Gerould, Chester Bennett, William Martin, and Ernest Smith.

The Wampum School, shown here in 1914, closed at the end of World War I and soon became the George W. MacInnis American Legion Post #225.

The Wrentham High School Class of 1921 included the following students, from left to right: (front row) Marion Pierce, Frances Jordan, Albert Locklin, Katherine Bullard, and Loretta Proteau; (back row) Cora Bell, Fred Cepurneek, and Lena Dombrowitz.

This photograph of the Wrentham High School Class of 1914 includes the following, from left to right: (front row) Ora Kenisto, Mary Winter, Ruth Miller, President Charles Perry, Loretta Holden, Ida May Bliek, and Ethel Cook; (back row) Gertrude Holden, Louise Brastow, Elsie Quirk, Howard Parker, Mae Cook, Dorothy Castleton, and Isabella Winter.

When the Center School at 55 East Street burned to the ground in February 1895, plans were immediately begun to construct the new Center School, shown here in its first year. The beautiful building became the center of many of Wrentham's activities for more than the next half century, housing the first through twelfth grades until 1936, when the George L. Vogel

School was completed for grades one through six and the new Center School became the junior-senior high. The new Center School also housed the town hall, and was the auditorium for school assemblies, school and other organizational plays, dances and proms, donkey basketball games, minstrel shows, and gym classes, among other activities.

This is the 1926 Wrentham High School girls' basketball team. From left to right are as follows: (front row) Ethel Raymond, Barbara Cook, and Catherine McGarry; (back row) Genevieve Nardelli, Gretchen Metcalf, Flora Postle, and coach Ruth Walker.

The Wrentham High School girls' basketball team of 1929 consisted of the following people, from left to right: (front row) Katherine Clark, Kay Hooper, and Joan Cashen; (back row) Coach Hapgood, Celia Shanker, Ethel Raymond, Ruby Jamieson, Madeleine Joyce, and Marguerite Holden.

The boys' basketball team of Wrentham High posed for a photograph in 1910. John A. Warren is to the extreme left in the front.

The Wrentham High School boys' basketball team of 1930 consisted of the following people, from left to right: (front row) Kenneth Youngdahl, Paul Giannetti, and Ernest Melbye; (back row) principal and coach Earle Swett, Loel Raymond, Richard Farrar, George Hoffman, and Ernest Hoffman.

This group picture of the entire student body of Wrentham High School was taken in 1929. They are, from left to right, as follows: (front row) Grace Coleman, Ruth Felch, Raymond George, Nelson Irving, Thomas Wood, Phillip Weber, Russell Young, Wilfred Rowell, and James S. Floyd: (second row) Howard Wheeler, William Pierce, Hugo Giannetti, Charles Davis, Gerald O'Leary, Donald Kirkton, Earle Stewart, Wilfrid Cashen, two unidentified students, Frank McGarry, and Crawford Lally; (third row) Leona Vary, Patricia Lynam, Dorothy Blaisdell, Frances Weber, Margaret Bennett, Dorothy Wheeler, Katherine Clark, Irma Vary, Merle Ware, Betty Shepardson, Marjorie Flowers, Martha Ellsworth, and Mary McCarty; (fourth row) Emily Roby, Barbara Willard, Madeleine Joyce, Lois Burgess, Carol Shaw, Eleanor Stringer, Celia Shanker, Ruth Jenkins, Ruby Jamieson, Dorothy Amlaw, Jean Cowell, Doris Sprague, and Bertha Fuller; (back row) Murray George, George Hoffman, John Miller, Richard Farrar, Willard Whipple, Verne Olsen, Edward McGarry, William Proctor, Ernest Hoffman, Enrigo Giannetti, Loel Raymond, Ernest Melbye, and Kenneth Youngdahl.

The Wrentham Junior High School basketball team is shown here in 1930. Among the players are Al Paquette, Kip Jenkins, Nelson Schaaf, Pete Bowman, Eddie Coyle, Coach Frederick Atkins, John Bishop, Norman Parkhurst, Hector Paquette, Bill Palmer, Billy Rowell, and Gus Colletto.

The Wrentham High School Class of 1941 included Richard Starkey, Sylvia Walton, Muriel Peatfield, Irving "Bud" Fisher, Lillian O'Heare, Mary Leonard, Ethel Winter, Miss Grace Whitaker (Faculty Advisor), Peggy Metcalf, Vera Saks, Doris Gould, and Elliott Armitage. Katherine Irving is missing from the photograph, as are Robert Enegren and Donald Carlander (who were sick with the mumps!).

In September 1935, the new George L. Vogel Elementary School opened. It originally contained six classrooms, only one room being required for each of the first six grades.

Some of these second graders were later members of the Wrentham High School Class of 1943. Included in this picture are Eugene Cobb, Henry Colletto, George Crosen, Joseph Duffy, Betty Gilmore, Peter Heffron, Robert Larsen, Harold Lockwood, John Metcalf, Ann Murphy, Barbara Nash, Betsy Parker, Edward Poles, Corinne Weinstein, Jeanne Wignall, Virginia Wignall, Henry Williams, Muriel Winter, Eleanor Woodhams, and Phyllis Young.

The older son, John H. Warren, of School Committee Chairman John A. Warren is about to raise the flag. The Sheldonville School still housed the first six grades of students from the west end of town at the time of this photograph. The Center School at the corner of Dedham and Franklin Streets was now accommodating grades seven through twelve for the whole town.

Several Center School teachers, including Gilbert Rishton, Priscilla Little, Doris Higginbottom, Harriet Dimmick, Lila Doe, Evelyn Dexter, Grace Whitaker, Earle Swett, are shown here in 1930.

This is how some of the Wrentham High School Class of 1946 looked in the fifth grade in the George L. Vogel School. They are, from left to right, as follows: (front row) Francis Hart, Ann Quinn, Marilyn Mitchell, Joan Cooney, Helen Aylward, Loretta Colletto, unknown, Elinor Young, and unknown: (middle row) unknown, John DeVisscher, unknown, Marion Bennett, Jean Buckley, Frances Fortier, Virginia Binney, Eleanor Campbell, Alan Tadgell, and Dean May; (back row) teacher Miss Esther Richardson, unknown, George Candela, Barbara Enegren, Barbara McNeil, Barbara Kelly, two unknown students, Albert Moreland, and George Irving.

This is a composite photograph of the Wrentham High School Class of 1944.

Class of 1945
Wrentham High School

Frank Jordan · David Newcomb · Gordon Woodham · Jeanne Peters · Donald Patten · Marjery Jenness · Marion Olson · Clara Candela · Ruth Roberts · Norma Hoyt · Thelma Larson · Frances Jordan · Ruth Shepard · Phyllis Fernand · Rita Barr · Calista Dibblee · Claire Davis · Ruth McNamara

Laura Lou Startz, V. Pres. · Richard Capron, Pres. · Louise Packard, Sec'y · Doris Hogarth, Treas.

Purdy, Boston

The Wrentham High School Classes of 1945 (above) and 1946 (below) were considerably larger than graduating classes had been even 30 years previous.

Class of 1946
Wrentham High School

Henry Wignall · Richard Moriarty · Marjorie Kelley · Howard Cook · Douglas Turner · Ann Quinn · Statia Lewicki · Marion Bennett · Lorraine Lustenberger · Elinor Young · Barbara McNeil

Loretta Colletto, President · Virginia Binney, Secretary · Barbara Heinz, Treasurer · George Candela, Vice-Pres.

Purdy, Boston

Doctor Charles Roderick was a longtime Wrentham "country doctor" who lived and worked out of 155 South Street, known as "The Doctors House," having been originally owned by Doctor George F. Butman and by five consecutive doctors following. Doctor Roderick was, for a time, the school doctor, and one elementary school has been named for him.

Esther Richardson White, a longtime teacher and administrator in Wrentham's school system, and her husband, Sidney, are seen greeting Dr. Roderick on the occasion of the dedication of the new Roderick School.

Dick Shepherd, the head baker at the Wrentham State School, looks over one of dozens of loaves of bread baked daily for consumption by the patients and staff. The bakery building provided all the necessary baked goods for the hundreds of meals served daily, as well as a meaningful activity for those patients capable of doing the work.

As state government settled down after the turmoil of World War I, the Wrentham State School, under the Department of Mental Health, continued with its task of expansion. The Industrial Building provided the necessary facilities for the patients to do a variety of meaningful tasks. The girls' industrial classes taught skills such as sewing and basket making.

This drawing by the firm of Kendall Taylor and Company shows the 1930 proposal and plans for the Wrentham State School campus.

Clearing the land and the subsequent farming, which provided fresh vegetables for patients and staff, also provided meaningful training and activities for many of the young men of the school.

102

Seven

THE HUMAN SIDE

The Wrentham State School's farm, grounds, and building maintenance staff gathered for this photo. Sitting in the center is Head Farmer John Woodhams, and to his left is Farm Supervisor Fred Heffron. Herb Smith and Thomas Coyle also appear in the image.

People are the heart of a community and the following photos show a few of those who have had some influence in the shaping of Wrentham today and will continue some influence for years to come, maybe forever. The pictures are not included to imply that some are more important than others, for each person must judge that for himself. We hope that this collection will cause each of you to reach back mentally, to reminisce and enjoy your own recollections of those who have had some influence on you.

Young George W. MacInnis shows off his fresh World War I army uniform. He served in France in Company I, 101st Infantry, and was killed in action on June 2, 1918. France awarded him the Croix de Guerre. He is buried in an unpretentious grave, to the left just inside the East Street entrance of the Center Cemetery (see p. 74).

Motorman Rodney Tyler proudly stands in front of his car. The poster on the front of the car advertises evening movies at Lake Pearl Park, and dancing every Tuesday, Thursday, and Saturday night.

On May 30, 1919, Wrentham held a massive celebration and called it "Welcome Home Day" to honor all those men and women returning home after World War I. General Clarence Edwards was a most prominent guest and the festivities were planned and headed by State Representative George Dodd and prominent businessman Patrick Mahoney.

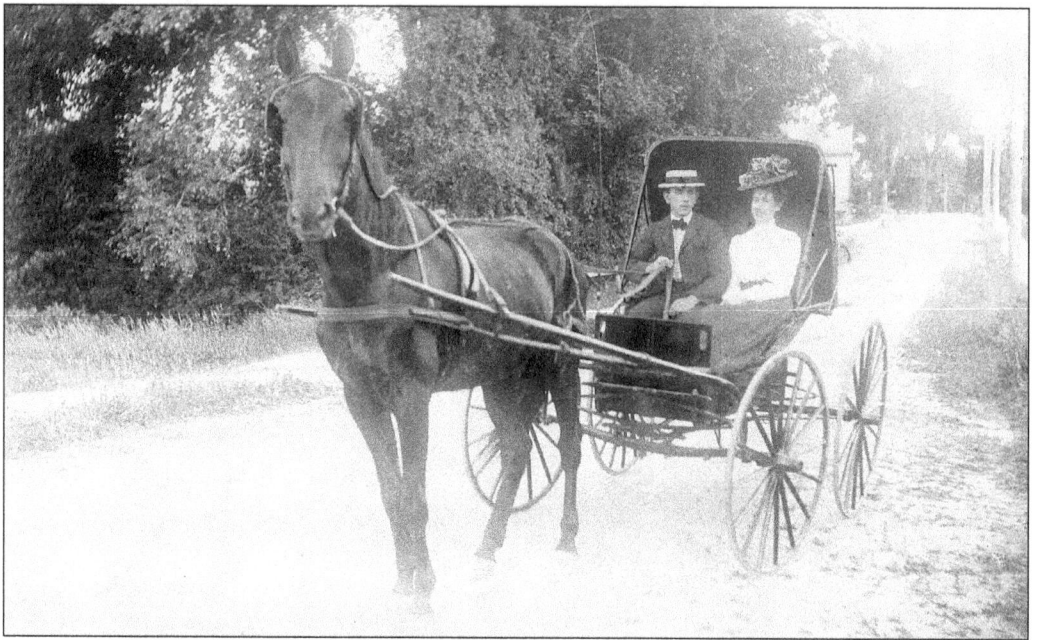

Walter H. Stewart, who was boarding at 95 East Street in 1904, directed "Teddy" to Wampum Corner to court Mary A. Follett and take her for a country ride. Walter and Mary were married the following year.

The chauffeur positioned Mr. William Sweatt's new 1904 White Steamer for a photograph as he prepared to take Mr. and Mrs. Sweatt for a ride in the country. Mr. Sweatt, Wrentham's longtime benefactor, originally lived in Norfolk but moved to 289 East Street about 1925. In his will in 1926 he bequeathed the property to the King's Daughters and Sons Home for the Aged, which replaced the Pond Home on Valley Street in Norfolk.

Tilting Rock was a favorite spot for Sunday picnics. Eighteen-year-old Grace Simpson Proctor is shown here in 1900 playfully pretending to be keeping the rock from tipping over. Today, chiseled into the southerly side, are several initials and the name of John Bishop, a casualty of World War II.

In the winter of 1896, Dr. Jenckes stood for a photograph on the sidewalk of the brand new town library, which was still called the "Wrentham Public Library," having not yet been renamed the Fiske Public Library. In the child's sled in front is one-year-old Charles Perry Sr.

Before town water was made available in 1910, rain water was often collected in cisterns or barrels. Hiram A. Cowell is shown here siphoning from a barrel located near the street car stop at the upper common. Note Daniel Cook's hall in the background.

Daniel S. Farrington, whose historic house was demolished by the town in 1951 to make room for a town building, must have been proud of the cast-iron fence at the front of his property since he posed there for photographs several times. Across the street at 82 South Street was John F. Shepard's dry goods store.

The market at about 48 South Street was, during the time of this photo in 1939, two stores. On the right is Sam Shanker's shoe store, and on the left is the A&P. Sam is standing in front, and behind him is Paul Danahy Sr., manager of the A&P. To Sam's right is Paul's brother-in-law, meat cutter Joe Middleton; to Sam's left is Ernie Hoffman.

Daniel S. Farrington, known as a reporter for the *Pawtucket Times*, stands with tax collector Frederick A. Shepard at the iron fence in front of Farrington's house.

Daniel Brown, born in Antrim, Ireland, came to this country with his father while still a young man. He bought George's straw shop business and after it burned to the ground in 1878, built a new Wrentham Straw Works behind his home on Common Street, and operated it until his death in 1904. His son Charles continued its operation until his untimely death at the age of 39. Charles' wife continued the business for only one year.

Civil War veteran Alonzo F. Bennett was born in West Wrentham in 1841. He worked for the Sturdy and Shephardson jewelry factory in Wrentham Village and in 1872 started a jewelry business in partnership with Charles Young as "Young and Bennett." In 1884 he married Mary A. Morss. At the time of his death in 1905, he owned the property at 458 South Street and other properties, including what is now Oak Point.

Wrentham's town baseball team lined up for these interesting photos in 1933, showing the team and its sponsors. From left to right are as follows: (front row) Milt Bennett, Tony Nardelli, Gus Colletto, Don Kirkton, and Cappie Blaisdell; (middle row) Rolly Francis, Howard Moulton, Cap Blaisdell, Rig Giannetti, Horace King, and Earl Waterman; (back row) Howard Morse, Al Morse, Fran Faulkner, Joe Cataldo, Tom Coyle, and Roy Jenness. In the photograph below, they've turned to reveal the sponsers who paid for the uniforms.

George Francis ran this store at 40 South Street from before 1908 until the business was bought by Clinton "Doc" Davis in 1937. It served as the ticket office for the electric street railroad, the New England and Greyhound bus lines, and was the town's only franchise dealer of Boston and New York newspapers.

These well-known "townies" got together for many activities before World War II including this photo. They are, from left to right, Gus Colletto, "Chick" Hatt, Dave Kennedy, Bill Palmer, Norm Parkhurst, Johnny Miller, "Co" Lally, and John Colletto. "Chick" Hatt and "Co" Lally never returned from the war.

Norfolk businessman William H. Sweatt died while on a trip to Italy in 1929, the result of a fall. His will left a significant amount of money in a trust for the benefit of the people of Wrentham and has provided innumerable benefits such as Sweatt Park, Sweatt Beach, the Sweatt Ski Slope, several athletic fields, and items and services for many town departments.

After her husband's death, Mrs. Sweatt was so despondent that one day she had her chauffeur drive her to her husband's grave, whereupon she took her own life.

The Trinity Church Men's Club ran a Saturday fair on the lower common for many years. Pictured here is part of the happy clean-up crew sweeping the area before 7 a.m. on a Sunday morning in the early 1950s. From left to right are John Kady, Bill Pierce, John Stobbart, and Bert Thompson.

Fred E. Gilmore, a prominent poultryman, lived at 332 South Street and was a director of the National Bank of Wrentham. His father-in-law, James E. Carpenter, was shot and killed in the November 1, 1924, during an attempted bank robbery.

The Reverend Melville A. Shafer was a minister for the original Congregational church for 32 years. He organized Wrentham's Boy Scouts and was the Wrentham correspondent for the *Franklin Sentinel* weekly newspaper.

Perley Dexter, shown here in his best chief's outfit, was chief of police from June 15, 1925, until his untimely death on June 10, 1937.

Hester Getchell Brown, the widow of Daniel Brown (who owned the Wrentham Straw Works), is pictured rocking her first grandchild, Hope H. Hall, in 1916. Hope lived her whole life in the family home at 36 Common Street and was the last surviving family member when she died in 1991.

Electric railroad motormen stopped long enough to allow a photographer to take their picture.

Eight

BUILDINGS

If the people are the heart a community and cause to happen those things that make it unique, it is the buildings that remain to remind us of the people who have been here before us. In New England, man needs protection from the weather, and the protection that he builds reflects his lifestyle, his means, his ingenuity, and often his artistic ability. The following photographs include several buildings that were here before the beginning of photography and many that have long ago disappeared due to natural causes, or often by demolition. Some have been preserved and they allow us, at times, to drift back, dreamily, to the time of our ancestors.

The second home of Troop D of the Massachusetts State Police in Wrentham, from 1930 to 1933, was this building at 194 Winter Street. Previous to this, from 1926 to 1930, it had been located on Dedham Street, when it was still Route 1. From the Winter Street location, Troop D moved into the 1810 house at the corner of the new Route 1 and Main Street in Foxboro. In 1937 it moved to what had been the Wrentham Poor Farm on East Street, and in 1957 it moved to its present home.

Shown as the town "asylum" on Walling's 1851 map of Wrentham, and as the town "poor farm" in the 1876 *Norfolk County Atlas*, this building served the town well into the 20th century as housing for people who were unable to care for themselves. From 1937 to 1956, the town rented it to the Massachusetts State Police, who quartered Troop D here, having outgrown the building on Dedham Street. The barn to the left was burned by the town as practice for firemen, and the house was demolished after the MSP moved to new quarters in Foxborough.

The Oliver Druce house at 21 East Street was sold to John Francoeur, a French Huguenot, in 1794. Count Louis de Cornette lived here, died, and was buried in Wrentham.

This house has had several well-known owners, including David Fisher, Handel Pond (the organist and deacon of the Congregational Church), and Charles Hamilton (a master mariner). Now owned by the church, it has been named "The Whiston House."

This 1902 house at 340 Franklin Street was once the home of Dr. George L. Vogel. Dr. Vogel served in World War I and was affiliated with the Boston Eye and Ear Infirmary. The 1935-36 elementary school was named in his honor by a majority vote at a town meeting.

This very early example of a colonial country farmhouse was the longtime home of the Hawes family, and the road became known as Hawes Street. The house was destroyed long ago.

The "Lightning Splitter" at 8 Shepard Street became well known in 1832 when, after several unsuccessful searches, a sheriff's posse "smoked out" a small band of counterfeiters. The single-story house, which featured a very steep roof, had three attics, the third one of which seemed to have no access and so had not been searched. One of the officers accidentally tossed some snuff into the large kitchen fireplace, causing one of the hidden counterfeiters to sneeze, giving their hiding place away. The building was destroyed by its owners.

The home of Judge Samuel Day was located at 996 West Street. Judge Day served Wrentham and his country in a number of ways during his life—he took part in the Revolutionary War under Capt. Lemuel Kollock's command, was a state representative from 1805 to 1808, served on the first bench of the Norfolk County Court in 1806, and was a state senator from 1809 to 1811.

In 1904 Daniel Brown built this home for his son, Charles E. "Eddy" Brown, in the front yard of the Wrentham Straw Works, which is visible in the background. Charles died of a ruptured appendix at the age of 39, and shortly thereafter his widow sold the house to Charles MacDougald, a cashier of the National Bank of Wrentham for many years.

This photograph was taken of 458 South Street about 1890, just before the new roadway was laid out. The rebuilding of the road required the removal of the stone wall, which was used for fill just down the road, and a sidewalk was added. Built by John Mady DeCoubulon in 1795, this house has been owned by Revolutionary War veteran Rufus Mann, county deputy sheriff Timothy Whitney, and Alonzo Bennett, a veteran of the Civil War. It is still owned by descendants of Alonzo Bennett.

Pondville Home
Pondville Mass.

This ancestral home was given by Virgil Pond in 1900 to the King's Daughters and Sons Home for the Aged and was dedicated on June 3, 1902, as the "Pond Home." The Reverend Edward Everett Hale was the speaker of the day. It remained as the Pond Home until 1933-34.

Knuckup Farm, built on this site in 1813, was remodeled in 1861. The Fales Box Manufacturing Company, a maker of boxes for the straw hat business, was located here when a devastating fire began on April 7, 1898. This was later the location of the Wrenmere Inn; in 1935, it became the site of the George L. Vogel Elementary School.

Four women are playing croquet on the lawn at 60 Common Street at its intersection with Taunton Street. The house, built in 1780, was sold by Daniel Hawes to Dr. James Mann, a Revolutionary War surgeon. The Curtis Stone family, proprietors of Stone and Son Store at 42 South Street, lived here for about 80 years; previous to their occupancy, Dr. Samuel Bugbee had lived here for 30 years.

Oliver Felt, a cabinetmaker, owned the house at 234 South Street. His son, Edmund J. Felt, later owned the house. In 1870 it was bought by Day's Academy graduate William Proctor, the son of Thomas Proctor.

This house was built for Amasa Bagley at 612 South Street *c.* 1800. Oliver Ruggles' widow, Charlotte, later willed it to Willard H. Bennett, a carpenter who worked for the Red Bird Farm and, for 27 years, as an assessor.

After moving from Norfolk, William Sweatt and his wife owned and lived at this house at 289 East Street. This is now the main front section of the Pond Home.

This house was built at 128–130 East Street by the two Rathbun brothers, Henry and Albert, who operated a sawmill together. They each owned their own half of the house and maintained it almost as two separate buildings.

The Rathbuns seemed to have made good use of "scrap" lumber, as evidenced by this photo of the solid wood walls, exposed by a motor vehicle accident that occurred a few years ago.

Early generations of the Gerould family came to Wrentham as French refugees. This home, built around 1860, belonged to Joseph B. Gerould, whose three daughters, Susan, Ellen, and Mary, taught school in Wrentham. In the 1950s, it was the Hitching Post Restaurant; it has since become the Wrentham Co-operative Bank.

Cook's Farm on West Street, now run by Warren and Marilyn Cook, has been in the family for ten generations. The farm's produce continues to be sold at the retail store in the adjacent barn.

Red Farm Wrentham Mass.

In 1906, this postcard picture of the Red Farm shows that the electric street cars were running between Wrentham and Franklin, and that the poultry farm had a wind-powered water pump to fill a sizable, elevated wooden water tank, somewhat of a luxury at that time.

TRINITY CHURCH   WRENTHAM MASSACHUSETTS
RECTOR   ALBERT HARRISON EWING
SERVICES   Sunday At 11·00
HOLY COMMUNION On Second Sunday
EVENING PRAYER AT 7·05 OCT TO JUNE

Young Reverend A. Harrison Ewing had this postcard printed in the early 1900s while rector of Trinity Church. He started a boys choir that included boys such as the Perry brothers of East Street, Howard Parker, and John A. Warren.